Joy of the Rosary

Joy of the Rosary

A Way into
Meditative Prayer

WOODCUTS BY DAVID M. JONES
PRAYERS BY CARYLL HOUSELANDER

ANNE VAIL

Liguori
LIGUORI, MISSOURI

Published by Liguori Publications
Liguori, Missouri

Library of Congress Cataloging-in Publication Data

Vail, Anne.
     Joy of the rosary : a way into meditative prayer / Anne Vail ; wood engrav-
ings by David Jones ; prayers by Caryll Houselander. — 1st U.S. ed.
          p. cm.
     ISBN 0-7648-0183-X
     1. Rosary. 2. Catholic Church—Prayer–books and devotions—English.
I. Houselander, Caryll. II. Vail, Anne. Rosary. III. Title.
BX2310.R7V35   1998
242'.74—dc21   97–34252
24

The prayers by Caryll Houselander in this book originally appeared in Maisie Ward's
The Splendor of the Rosary, published by Sheed & Ward, 1945.

First published in 1997 by The Canterbury Press Norwich, Norwich, Norfolk, Great
Britain, under the title *The Rosary: A Way Into Prayer*.

Scripture quotations are from the *New Revised Standard Version of the Bible*, copyright
© 1989 by the Division of Christian Education of the National Council of the
Churches of Christ in the USA. Used with permission. All rights reserved.

98 99 00 01 02 5 4 3 2 1
Printed in the United States of America

Contents

~ PART ONE ~

The Beads

❧ CHAPTER 1 ❧

The Circlet of Beads

The name "ROSARY" is given to the small circlet of beads which is so familiar to its devotees as to be taken for granted, although to some people it is a rather strange relic of a bygone age. The very simplicity of most rosaries, crammed into laden pockets, gives them a matter-of-fact image, rather like a key ring or a fountain pen. They are part of the "luggage" of many Catholics and other Christians. Even those who may have only a muddled idea of the prayer of the rosary still carry their beads, as if the small circlet provides some sort of spiritual insurance.

The word "bede" originally meant "prayer," and to "bid one's bedes" was a literal reference to saying one's prayers. In the sixteenth century, the word "bede" or "bead" was freed from its religious association, but by then the word "rosary" had come to refer to the circlet of beads with which we are familiar.

But why do we need to count our prayers anyway? It is hard to find any area of human activity that we do not seek to quantify. Some of us seem to be almost obsessed with numbers and seem curiously satisfied with any statement that is backed up by a statistic. Prayer can be the most elusive and frustrating activity as well as the most sublime experience, and there is no reason why it, too, should not be subject to our desire for order and regulation. Sometimes we need to count our prayers in order to know how many we have said and where we are in the sequence of the prayer we are saying.

Ways of counting prayer were very important to Christians of the eleventh century, many of whom participated in the daily monastic prayer which included the recitation and chanting of the 150 psalms. The abbeys were the centers of learning, and few people beyond the walls of the monasteries were able to read or write. Those who came in from the villages and fields to join the monks at prayer might have been reduced to being little more than onlookers if someone had not had the bright idea of tying 150 knots in a length of string. With the help of this practical device laypeople were able to recite the Pater Noster (Our Father) in response to each of the 150 Psalms. The origin of the expression "pitter patter" is said to come from the sound of their whispered prayer.

On their return from Jerusalem and the east, the medieval crusaders brought glowing accounts of prayer beads they had seen in use among the Muslims, and their reports influenced the development of different types of prayer beads in Europe. The custom of counting prayers on beads had therefore been in existence long before the rosary became popular in the fourteenth century.

In 1041, William of Malmesbury presents us with evidence of the first recorded use of beads for prayer, apart from the counting of Pater Nosters. He describes the beads of Lady Godiva as a circlet of threaded jewels on which she was accustomed to number her prayers in honor of the Blessed Virgin and which she bequeathed to be hung around the neck of the statue of Mary in the church at Coventry where she lived.

In fourteenth-century England, prayer beads were given the name "rosary," for the rose was not only the symbol of Our Lady but of England itself. Devotion to Mary had become part of English culture, and England had come to be known as Our Lady's Dowry. Although this title fell into comparative disuse, it has never been relinquished—and the rose remains the symbol of England.

Until the Reformation in the sixteenth century, roses were woven into chaplets or crowns that would be placed on statues of Mary on her feast days. The connection was strengthened by biblical allusion: "I am the rose of Sharon" (Song 2:1), and "I grew tall...like rosebushes in Jericho" (Sirach 24:14). Rose gardens became an accepted image of paradise, and in monastic gardens the "paradise" was cultivated by the monks.

As prayer beads became popular, the rich spent vast sums on threaded jewels, and the courts of Europe positively sparkled with the rosaries of the nobility.

Today, we are increasingly aware of the finite nature of the world's resources and are able to treasure natural materials. The quality of wood or of glass can be almost as precious to us as the jewels of a previous age. Modern prayer beads are generally more sober and discreet than in earlier days and echo the knots of string used by medieval Christians. We seem to have come full circle and rediscovered that the basic role of prayer beads is to help us count our prayers. They are of course of secondary importance to the prayer itself.

~ CHAPTER 2 ~

Our Lady's Psalter

*T*HE PRAYER OF THE ROSARY IS THOUGHT TO HAVE EVOLVED IN THE THIRTEENTH CENTURY FROM THE TEACHING OF SAINT DOMINIC, who traveled from Castille in Spain to the Languedoc in the south of France in 1206. There Dominic and his companions spent several years preaching to people suffering the indoctrination of a heretical sect known as the Albigensians, named after the town of Albi where they had established themselves. Albigensianism was an updated version of a far older heresy known as Manicheism, a creed of despair.

All that was material and human was vilified in the teaching of the Albigensians. Instead of seeing life and the human body as gifts of a loving God, and the world in which he placed us as a source of beauty and the means of sustaining life, everything bodily and material was viewed as an evil from which human beings should turn with loathing. The real meaning of life was lost, and the resulting desolation frequently led to suicide.

Because the Albigensians utterly rejected the New Testament narrative of Christ's life, and their doctrine was based on the perpetual conflict between spirit and flesh, Saint Dominic especially spoke to the Albigensians of the Incarnation. He stressed the great love of God, who sent his only Son into the world to die for our sins in order that we might be reunited with him.

Dominic's teaching was based on biblical wisdom infused with love. Piercing the belief system of the Albigensians was an immense task that could only be accomplished through the grace of Dominic's profound spirituality. His listeners were touched not only by the elaborate logic Dominic put forth, but above all by the power of prayers that he uttered.

Since all that was part of bodily experience was held to be evil, what more effective means could be used to touch the hearts of the people than promoting the unceasing contemplation of Christian virtues as expressed in the lives of the holy family. The prayers Dominic recited as an accompaniment to this contemplation were the Our Father, the prayer that Jesus taught us, the Hail Mary, the oldest and simplest of Christian salutations, and the Gloria, the acknowledgment prayer that all honor is due to him who created the universe. By reciting these most familiar of prayers, the mind was able, without wandering, to hold on to the truth of the scene being contemplated and to understand its meaning. Thus, the three significant prayers that would eventually be included in the rosary were used by Dominic as aids to contemplation.

Before the name "rosary" came into general use, this form of prayer was widely known as Our Lady's Psalter because the 150 Hail Marys to be recited reflected the 150 Psalms in the Bible.

By its division into fifteen parts, each commemorating an event in the life of our Lord and the Blessed Virgin, Saint Dominic sought to impress the Scripture narrative more deeply into the minds and hearts of his listeners so that each scene became more vivid and palpably real.

We know that the prayer of the rosary evolved into the form we know today during the thirteenth century, a time when devotion to the Blessed Virgin had a practical, earthy approach. The words of the Song of Songs, "a garden locked, a fountain sealed," were taken to heart, for they symbolized the womb that bore the Redeemer. And to Saint Dominic who, according to his thirteenth-century chronicler Bernard Gui "glowed with the fervor of his devotion to the Virgin Mother of God," the true answer to the Albigensians was to be found in the image of the holy family and the miracle of the Incarnation.

Nowadays the rosary is generally divided into three groups of fifteen Hail Marys—the Joyful Mysteries, the Sorrowful Mysteries and the Glorious Mysteries.

Many people find it difficult to accept the repetitive nature of the prayer of the rosary, but the repetition of rhythm is an essential part of our lives. Indeed, our entire being and existence is subject to repetition. All that surrounds us moves in unceasing rhythm, as the sun rises and sets, the seasons follow one another, and growth is sustained by their sequence. The pulse of life itself is defined by constant movement. There can be something profoundly soothing in the repetition of words when we realize that those same words have been repeated daily for some eight centuries. If the rosary had merely been a prayer of mindless repetition, it would surely have ceased to hold any attraction long ago.

The Buddhist idea of a mantra is sometimes thought of in connection with the rosary. Since this idea is defined as a series of words that are recited as a support for meditation and concentration, there is a compelling reason for this association.

The rosary has been compared to the image of a child sitting on his mother's lap, fingering the beads of her necklace and murmuring to her while she turns the pages of a book before his eyes. The rosary is a prayer based on meditation on the life of Christ as described in the New Testament, with Mary as our guide and "reader."

The first cycle of the rosary contains the Joyful Mysteries, which deal with the events surrounding the serene yet overshadowed youth of Jesus. The Sorrowful Mysteries follow his passion from the garden of Gethsemane to death on the cross. The third cycle, the Glorious Mysteries, portray the Resurrection, the Ascension, the descent of the Holy Spirit, and finally the Assumption of Mary and her Coronation in heaven.

We enter this quiet and holy world with the help of the Blessed Virgin, who witnessed so many of these events: "His mother treasured all these things in her heart" (Luke 2:51). These beautiful words from the Gospel of Luke give the impression that much of what happened was not readily, or at least not immediately, understood even by Mary.

Catechisms have described a mystery as a revealed truth which is beyond our reason. The mention of the word "mystery" is something that immediately alerts and intrigues the mind, as any writer or reader of detective stories is aware. Although we know in faith that some things are beyond our understanding, this knowledge does not stop us from exploring the possibilities.

Obviously, we will never be able to understand fully the truths of faith because we are finite while God is infinite. But some small reflection of the glory of God can nevertheless be glimpsed, for example, in the complexity and beauty of nature. Such glimpses can prompt us to wonder at the mind of the Creator by whom all is sustained, although the actual reality is far beyond our comprehension.

To mystics like Saint Francis of Assisi, the hand of the Creator was vividly present in his creation, and Francis speaks joyfully of "brother sun" and "sister moon." Perhaps we, too, can catch a glimpse of his vision through the mysteries of the rosary in which we see not only the truths of our destiny in the grand sense, but on a more mundane level we can gain a sense of proportion in the midst of the muddle of our lives. Even those events we may count as nothing can assume an immense value as we see the hand of the Holy Spirit moving quietly through all that we do and all that happens to us.

A friend once told me that while meditating on the mysteries of the rosary, he first placed himself in his mind within the scene that was taking place, so that when the angel Gabriel appeared to Mary at the Annunciation, my friend quietly seated himself in the shadows and watched. The event became more astonishing and moving each time he did this. Imagining himself present at each of the Joyful Mysteries of the rosary, he saw the serenity of the life of the holy family, the courage and trust of Our Lady and Saint Joseph; the patience and loyalty of Simeon and Anna as they waited in the Temple, and the fear of Mary and Joseph when they lost their Child, only to find him in the Temple surrounded by the elders.

The Sorrowful Mysteries became for him the image of a turbulent world, of cruelty and cowardice. He watched the despair and loneliness of the scene in the garden of Gethsemane, the mindless brutality of the soldiers and the crowd, the compassion shown to the grieving women, the courage of Veronica and Simon of Cyrene, and ultimately the loneliness and desolation of the cross. Among the images passing before him in his imagination, one constantly recurred. In sixteenth- and seventeenth-century paintings, Mary has so often been portrayed as a figure weeping and swooning with grief at the foot of the cross. Saint John says simply that she stood at the foot of the cross. The image of the figure of Mary standing unflinching before the dying figure of her Son, standing in humility, prayer, and silence, stands as the model for every Christian.

The Glorious Mysteries can appear as an extraordinary example of human bewilderment in the face of the workings of heaven. We are led through the incredulous visits to the empty tomb, the unspeakable joy of the apostles as the truth finally dawns on them that Jesus has indeed risen and is among them once more. At the descent of the Holy Spirit and the foundation of the Church, they are filled with courage and holiness. Finally comes the coronation of the Blessed Virgin in heaven which is the fulfillment of the promise given to us all, "I will come again and will take you to myself, so that where I am, there you may be also" (John 14:3). These momentous events find an echo in our everyday lives and cannot leave us untouched. As we meditate on the mysteries of the rosary, we recognize familiar faces and perceive events that recur in our lives, even though in different guises. All this is brought to mind through the gentle repetition of the Hail Mary as we enter a world in which our thoughts move with freedom limited only by the gentle rhythm of prayer.

Catechisms describe prayer as the "raising up of the mind and heart to God," and the prayer of the rosary is an example of the path of prayer. We turn our thoughts to the Scriptures and in calling to mind any event from the life of Christ as portrayed in the Gospels we can only become aware of his compassion, his gentleness with repentant sinners, his meekness, and his humility. As these become increasingly evident, we can hardly remain indifferent.

CHAPTER 3

A Prayer for All Occasions

I T IS VIRTUALLY IMPOSSIBLE TO DWELL ON THE ACCOUNTS OF THE GOSPELS FOR ANY LENGTH OF TIME WITHOUT BEING SWEPT UP INTO their truth and with one's heart remaining untouched. This response is not merely the stuff of dramatic revelation but a means of inspiring us to live by this extraordinary teaching that holds out the promise of the peace for which we so long.

But so often our prayer is a garbled plea, snatched at in moments of distress or need, knowing that God understands the turmoil of our lives. And yet we know that we need periods of silence; we need to stop for our spirits to draw breath. And perversely this is something that we put off—almost as if we fear that, having once achieved calm, we will not know what to do next. The mere effort of relaxing causes the greatest stress of all.

The world is full of ingenious recipes for meditation and new forms of recreation. And yet the true meaning of the word is "re-creation," the created turning to its Creator. What could be more natural, more vital and, to be honest, more daunting? It is all too easy to misconstrue this glaring need of the soul and to become discouraged.

We are obsessed with the care of our physical bodies. The need for diet and exercise has become almost a religion in itself. The mere suggestion of the damaging effect of pollution on our food can send us into a spiral of panic. And yet the needs of the spirit remain overlooked, and we are ill-prepared even to undertake the task of discerning those needs. We feel that it should happen naturally and when it fails to do so, we are disheartened. Subconsciously, we seem to realize the importance of prayer but fail to understand that it is a fundamental part of life. It is as if we are in awe of some august acquaintance, whom we treat with circumspection and shyness, until we come to know that person and, through knowledge, begin to love him or her and eventually cannot imagine life without this person. Ignorance turns many of us away from prayer, and the deepest ignorance lies in our misunderstanding of prayer itself. We can sometimes imagine that by means of immense effort and concentration we can achieve great things, but this very misconception dooms us to disappointment and failure.

Saint Paul teaches that we are the temple of the Holy Spirit (1 Corinthians 3:16–17), that the Spirit exists within each one of us. We have only to be quiet and listen. We have that wonderful description of the first prayer, God and Adam and Eve "walking in the garden at the time of the evening breeze" (Genesis 3:8), and it conjures up the intimacy of friend talking to friend.

When we are with a friend and cannot find the right words, we have only to be silent, and in the silence we can listen. The character of the prayer of the rosary was defined by Saint Dominic's own form of prayer which consisted of long periods of contemplative silence interrupted only by moments of speech, almost as if he were involved in deep conversation with his Lord. Sometimes his monks would see him thus in rapt attention, on occasion with his head to one side as if listening intently to someone who was addressing words of profound importance to him.

In quiet prayer we frequently find that an echo of our anxieties disturbs and distracts us, rather as one suddenly hears the tick of a clock which has been unnoticed in the general noise, but becomes insistent when silence descends. The world around us is one huge distraction. We are buffeted from one anxiety to another. It is strange to find in the Middle East that many people finger beaded strings that look like rosaries as a means of allaying stress and anxieties. These are in fact called "worry beads." In a way, these worry beads are akin to the rosary in the sense that it can be used as an aid to conquer distractions. In time we learn to ignore the easy lure of distractions—even without the mechanical aid of the rosary beads—but, even so, there is no doubt that meditative prayer requires practice.

The rosary is of immense value to the learned and unlearned alike, for it can be a great intellectual exercise to those who wish to reflect on the heights of human behavior, and the ultimate wisdom and mercy of an omnipotent God—an exercise that has taken the lifetime of many saints. At the same time, it is a means of immense and simple comfort, but in either case it is a source of great spiritual strength.

It may seem at first that in order to say the rosary at all, one needs the skill of a juggler to finger the beads, recite the prayers and meditate. And yet there are many far more complicated sequences that we perform. Driving a car involves steering, changing gears, remaining attentive to the road ahead, and keeping a wary eye on the other traffic. Yet we are quite capable of chatting to a companion in the passenger seat.

The rosary is especially the prayer for young parents beset by anxiety and exhaustion and aware of every danger awaiting their children as they grow up in a world alien to innocence. This prayer is infinitely flexible, a decade may be said at any time of day, waiting in a line or in the silence of the night beside a sleepless child. The compassionate figure of Mary overwhelms us with her solicitude and love, and protects us, all the while exhorting her son for his kindness on our behalf.

CHAPTER 4

The Heart of the Rosary

*T*HE FIGURE OF MARY HAS LONG BEEN HONORED AS MOTHER IN THE CHURCHES OF EAST AND WEST. IN THE EAST HER TITLE OF "GOD-bearer" (Theotokos) differs only slightly from the appellation of "Mother of God" which is more familiar in the west. The remote, almond-eyed yet serene figures of Orthodox iconography, the ornate masterpieces of the Renaissance and the mysterious black madonnas of the south of France all testify to our fascination with Mary as mother of God and of humankind. Yet the inspiration we receive from such human interpretations of Mary is obviously dependent upon the hand of the artist.

We have woven endless legends and wonders around the person of Mary because the ordinary Christian needs to find a means of expressing the weightier judgments of theologians. Some images, statues, and mementos give rise to disapproval but are nevertheless the reminder of a beloved ideal. Who has not gazed on the picture of a loved friend with wistful longing, while remaining perfectly well aware that it is not the picture one loves, but the reality it represents? The value of the picture lies in its ability to focus our attention and to make it easier to bring to mind the face of the living person. For this reason so many of our churches are filled with a happy muddle of statues and pictures. In the same way that we fill our homes with pictures of those whom we love, so we feel as we step from the busy pavement into the quiet of a church that we are entering into the company of the saints. The mind is instantly focused.

In the Middle Ages when most people were unable to read, visual explanations were used in order to clarify theological teaching. Numerous pictures related different aspects of the life of Our Lord in complex detail, and many again explained the different roles of the Virgin. In one of these pictures, known as the "Mantle of Grace," Mary is standing with her arms outstretched over an anxious multitude that is huddling beneath her star-strewn cape. She pleads on their behalf, reminding her Son that he received his own humanity from her. It is a wonderfully practical explanation of the role of Mary as intercessor and, at the same time, a vivid portrayal of complex theology. To many, this picture demonstrates the reality of the Church and at the same time the holiness that can encompass the vulnerability of humankind. The words "Hail, full of grace" sum up the attitude of the Catholic Church to Mary. Despite the brief, almost allusive, mention made in the Scriptures of the Blessed Virgin, she has been the sign of Christian mercy and humanity from the earliest times.

In the catacombs, Mary is portrayed as the young mother, symbol of the young Church: the praying heart in whom the identity of the Church is realized. For the Church finds its beginning in the faith of Our Lady at the Annunciation. As she bears the holy child, so she bears the mystery of salvation within her.

In his poem *The Blessed Virgin Compared to the Air We Breathe*, Gerard Manley Hopkins has described the mystery of the Incarnation in this way:

> So God was God of old
> A mother came to mould
> Those limbs like ours which are
> What must make our daystar
> Much dearer to mankind
> Whose glory would blind
> Or less would win man's mind
> Through her we may see him
> Made sweeter, not made dim
> And her hand leaves his light
> Sifted to suit our sight

This mystery of the Incarnation is the heart of the rosary. The sequence of meditations slowly unravels this deepest of mysteries which communicates salvation. By dwelling on each mystery we are drawn into a vision of divine love, in the company of Our Lady, as she represents the intended union of humanity with God, for in her sinless state she is the perfection of God's creation.

The experience of centuries endorses our allegiance to Mary.

She holds out a vision of peace and reassurance, of hope and trust in the eternal values, and ultimately of life over death. She shows us that she is the perfect example of human obedience, courage, and faith. We feel gratitude toward her which deepens into affection when the inspiring cause of that gratitude is understood. This affection can only deepen the reverence we show to her. In the eighth and ninth centuries, Mary was seen as chosen by God, pure and chaste, the mediator of the whole world when it was in danger, and especially at the hour of each person's death. For who can really remain calm in the face of our last uncertainty? Furthermore, in this century, Pope John Paul has consecrated the whole world to the protection of Mary.

Despite the solemnity of the subject of Mary as our protectress at death's door, there are pictures from earlier days which relate with a light and almost humorous touch, precisely how Our Lady was prepared to deal with such a situation. One such picture known as the *Scales of Justice* depicts Saint Michael, the heavenly judge, standing in all his awesome majesty, gazing into infinity, unaware of a poor soul, recently dead, looking anxiously up at him. In his hand, Saint Michael holds aloft the scales of justice: on one side, the scale of good, which looks ominously empty; and on the other, the scale of sins, which not only appears well filled but, to the horror of the poor soul, its weight is increased by a series of little devils pulling it further down. In the background, unseen by the anxious soul, stands the figure of the Blessed Virgin dropping her rosary beads one by one into the scale of good, so that to the undisguised amazement of the poor soul, his good deeds satisfactorily come to outweigh his wrongdoings. This scene does not merely represent a case of wishful thinking, for much Marian theology is portrayed in this picture.

⊶ CHAPTER 5 ⊷

The Rosary—
Yesterday
and Today

INSPIRING EXAMPLES OF THE DEVOTION OF THE PEOPLE OF EN-
GLAND AND SCOTLAND TO THE BLESSED VIRGIN MARY AND THE
prayer of the rosary appear in accounts of those who died on the scaffold
for their faith at the time of the penal laws during the sixteenth and
seventeenth centuries. At that time in England and Scotland, recitation of the rosary could invite imprisonment, torture, and even
death.

One Baron Idus of Eckelsdorff was on his travels in Scotland in 1615, and while in Glasgow he came upon the execution of John Ogilvie. The scene might have been of merely passing interest, for the Baron held no particular religious views at the time. As the condemned man bade farewell to his friends from the scaffold, he tossed his rosary beads into the crowd. To Eckelsdorff's immense surprise, they fell into his hands.

He was immediately surrounded by a clamoring crowd, and in an attempt to free himself, he quickly relinquished the beads and left the scene. For many years the memory haunted him, and eventually he turned to the Church and was converted. He then thought longingly of John Ogilvie's rosary: "If I could now get possession of it, I would spare no cost and I would keep it in gold when I got it." But the opportunity never presented itself again.

For many people today their rosary beads are among their most precious possessions. In times of grave illness, the beads are frequently held in acknowledgment of the forgiveness of Christ and the compassion of Our Lady. In times of great sorrow, they are held as comfort.

One of the effects of the fragmentation of the Catholic Church in the sixteenth century was the loss of importance given to Our Lady. The reforming Protestants risked losing much that was gentle and compassionate in Christ's message when devotion to Our Lady diminished. The results of such diminishment are far reaching, for experience shows that when devotion to the Blessed Virgin is overlooked, there is frequently a misunderstanding of the Incarnation. One of the many resulting tragedies is the loss of that almost "domestic" holiness which Mary inspires in family life. Her presence in the family as the mother of God emphasizes that the family is the Church in miniature.

Without this recognition, men and women are in danger of relinquishing the vision of holiness which can be theirs in a truly Christian marriage; the role of motherhood loses its ideal, and the sanctity of life itself may be questioned. For this reason, the rosary is the special prayer of the family. The late Father Patrick Peyton's expression, "the family that prays together stays together," is frequently used as evidence of the immense blessing to be gained from family prayer.

The vigilance of Our Lady embraces the whole of humanity. When danger threatens she has frequently appeared in different parts of the world—in France, Portugal, Yugoslavia, South America, and numerous other places. Wherever she appears, the message is the same: she calls for penance and prayer and, above all, for the prayer of the rosary which turns our hearts and souls toward the life, death, and Resurrection of her Son and ultimately toward peace.

Above all, the prayer of the rosary makes sense of our past, gives value to the present, and enables us to face the future with trust in God's love. It is the great prayer of Christian unity. By praying the rosary we are brought nearer to God, and through a greater understanding of the mysteries of the Scriptures, light is shed on the mystery of our own lives.

PART TWO

The Rosary Prayer

CHAPTER 6

Praying the Rosary

LTHOUGH SOME RELIGIOUS ORDERS, SUCH AS THE REDEMPTORISTS AND THE DOMINICANS, STILL CARRY CIRCLETS OF 150 beads, most rosaries now are made up of five decades, or five groups of ten beads, each decade being separated by a larger bead, either square or round, to emphasize the difference.

Attached to the circlet of beads there is a crucifix on a small chain containing first a single bead, and then three beads together in succession, followed by another single bead. To begin the recitation of the rosary, the crucifix is grasped in the hand, and with it the Sign of the Cross is made:

In the name of the Father, and of the Son, and of the Holy Spirit. Amen.

The Apostles' Creed is next recited on the crucifix, so we begin, at the outset, by making an affirmation of our belief.

I believe in God, the Father almighty, creator of heaven and earth. I believe in Jesus Christ, his only Son, our Lord. He was conceived by the power of the Holy Spirit and born of the Virgin Mary. He suffered under Pontius Pilate, was crucified, died, and was buried; he descended to the dead. On the third day he rose again. He ascended into heaven and is seated at the right hand of the Father. He will come to judge the living and the dead. I believe in the Holy Spirit, the holy catholic Church, the communion of saints, the forgiveness of sins, the resurrection of the body, and the life everlasting. Amen.

The Creed is followed, on the next single bead, by the Our Father:

Our Father, who art in heaven, hallowed be thy name; thy kingdom come; thy will be done on earth as in heaven. Give us this day our daily bread, and forgive us our trespasses as we forgive those who trespass against us; and lead us not into temptation, but deliver us from evil. (For the kingdom, the power, and the glory are yours, now and forever.) Amen.

The Our Father is followed by three Hail Marys recited on the three beads on the short chain following the crucifix. These are offered either for the gifts of faith, hope, and charity or sometimes for the grace of devout and uninterrupted prayer.

> *Hail Mary, full of grace. The Lord is with thee. Blessed art thou among women, and blessed is the fruit of thy womb, Jesus. Holy Mary, Mother of God, pray for us sinners, now and at the hour of our death. Amen.*

The Prayer of Praise is recited on the final single bead on the small chain connected to the crucifix:

> *Glory to the Father, and to the Son, and to the Holy Spirit; as it was in the beginning, is now, and will be for ever. Amen.*

Some people also say the Jesus Prayer along with the Prayer of Praise:

> *O my Jesus, forgive us our sins, save us from the fires of hell. Lead all souls to heaven, especially those who have most need of thy mercy. Amen.*

Recall the mystery for the first decade, and begin with the Our Father on the single, large bead, followed by ten Hail Marys on the smaller beads, and ending with the Prayer of Praise (and Jesus Prayer, if so desired). This cycle completes one decade. All the other decades are said in the same manner with a different mystery meditated upon during each decade. At the end of the rosary, the prayer Hail, Holy Queen may be recited:

> *Hail, holy queen, mother of mercy, our life, our sweetness, and our hope. To you we cry, poor banished children of Eve;*

to you we send up our sighs, mourning and weeping in this valley of tears. Turn then, O most gracious advocate, your eyes of mercy toward us, and after this our exile, show unto us the blessed fruit of your womb, Jesus. O clement, O loving, O sweet virgin Mary.

Pray for us, O holy Mother of God.

Response: *That we may be made worthy of the promises of Christ.*

Let us pray: *O God, whose only begotten Son, by his life, death, and Resurrection, has purchased for us the rewards of eternal life, grant, we beseech you, that meditating upon these mysteries of the most holy rosary of the Blessed Virgin Mary, we may imitate what they contain and obtain what they promise. Through the same Christ our Lord. Amen.*

Conclude the recitation of the rosary with the Sign of the Cross, again using the crucifix that anchors the beads.

Though there are many ways of reciting the rosary, it still remains a most practical prayer because it studies the life led by Jesus, who became man precisely to show us how we should lead our own lives.

We may feel that contemplation is the prerogative of those in religious life and is too complicated for us. Our thoughts may be confused by tomes of instruction that make us too worried to think about God. But it is really very simple, for to contemplate is to gaze with the mind held in stillness. Some of the Orthodox icons have this stillness about them that prompts the raising of the heart through the mind. The rosary allows for that silence and stillness which is essential to prayer.

There is a sense of rhythm in this prayer that in earlier times was usually recited in procession. And there is no doubt that, even today, reciting the rosary while walking, beads in the pocket or held in the hand, is a most natural and satisfying way of prayer. The rhythmic movement of walking so perfectly matches the pace of the words that it is reminiscent of early piano lessons with a metronome ticking out its sedate rhythm. In the same way, as our hand moves along the beads, our movement itself becomes prayer and, without realizing it, we become entirely occupied, mind and body, in praise of God. For some people, the rhythmic nature of the prayer suggests song. In France, the Hail Marys are frequently sung, the melody becoming like a love song, and the theme of the Incarnation and the love of the Blessed Virgin for her Son becomes the bridge between heaven and earth. All the mysteries celebrated in the rosary are, in reality, based on the single theme of the Incarnation.

A friend once told me of her busy urban parish where the congregation was so cosmopolitan that the rosary became almost unintelligible with so many different languages, accents, and intonations. The problem was solved by having each person in turn recite one decade in his or her own mother tongue. This resulted in a rosary made up of a decade in French, one in Spanish, and perhaps one in Vietnamese. On other occasions, the rosary was recited in Latin, for although Latin has ceased to be the official language of the Catholic liturgy, it remains a universal language of worship.

Another friend told me that he recited his most rewarding decades while sitting on a crowded bus or stalled in his car in traffic jams. As he prayed, his eyes would take in those around him, the lonely and sad, those whose faces were filled with despair, and he would offer his prayer for them.

It is interesting to return to the origins of the rosary to discover that we are not breaking new ground in seeking different ways of reciting the prayer. It has long been the custom to add clauses to the Hail Mary that refer to the theme of the mystery being contemplated. For example:

> *Hail Mary, full of grace. The Lord is with thee. Blessed art thou among women, and blessed is the fruit of thy womb, Jesus—whom you did conceive of the Holy Spirit—Holy Mary, Mother of God, pray for us sinners, now and at the hour of our death.*

Another example might be taken from the mystery of the Crucifixion when we might add, "...and blessed is the fruit of thy womb, Jesus—*who is dying on the cross before you.*" This custom follows a way of praying the rosary in Germanic countries, even for public recitation; a clause commemorating the mystery being contemplated for that particular decade is interpolated in each Hail Mary.

By using this form of the rosary, we can underline the theme of the mystery either elaborately or quite simply. For example, at the nativity mystery, we might say "...blessed is the fruit of thy womb, Jesus—*who lies in the manger.*" Or at the finding in the Temple, we might say, "...Holy Mary, Mother of God, pray for us now—*that we may also find Jesus.*" There are many ways in which we can adapt this method without altering the rhythm of our prayer. Each person will find his or her own words.

This method of inserting a focal point in the Hail Mary can be used in an even more intimate way. We might stop at the words "Holy Mary, Mother of God, pray for us now..." and add, "*when we most need your help....*" By using this form of prayer, we can underline the theme of the mystery either elaborately or quite simply.

In another adaptation, called the Scripture rosary, a short quotation is read from the Scriptures before each Hail Mary. This becomes a wonderful way of exploring the depth of each mystery, and uniting the gospels to the rosary prayer.

All of these methods obviously make the prayer much slower. But since the rosary is, above all, a prayer of meditation, the number of "extra" meditations may surely vary. We may decide to choose just one decade to dwell upon and expand, instead of elaborating on all the decades at one prayer sitting.

In the eighth and ninth centuries, both the Venerable Bede and Saint Aelred, abbot of Rievaulx, included the angel's first words, "Hail, full of grace" in their prayer, for the final "Holy Mary, Mother of God, pray for us…" was not added until the fifteenth century. We might follow their example and recite the angelic salutation, and go no further. Another variation, one that is especially useful if we are preoccupied, is to decide to choose an event from the New Testament that has particular significance for our state of mind and to dwell on it for the entire rosary.

The rhythm of the rosary is maintained in the sequence of the days of the week chosen for the different mysteries or themes from salvation history. Different days became associated with different themes. In one scheme, Monday traditionally became the day of the week consecrated to the angels. This happy celebration led to the saying of the Joyful Mysteries on Monday. Soon Thursday became a day associated with the Blessed Sacrament, and thus the Joyful Mysteries were said on Thursdays as well. Tuesday is the day of the apostles, and Friday is the day of the Crucifixion. These, then, are the days allocated to the saying of the Sorrowful Mysteries. The Glorious Mysteries are said on Saturday, traditionally the day of Our Lady, Sunday, the most sacred day of the week, and Wednesday, the day of the Holy Spirit.

Different themes for different days of the week grew up in different places. So, whatever mysteries we commemorate on specific days of the week, and however we decide to recite the rosary, the words of Scripture still create the "picture" on which we meditate. In the words of Saint Benedict, we listen "with the ears of the heart." We come as we are and let the Holy Spirit within us move us to speak to Our Lady as to a friend.

The Joyful Mysteries are taken up with family life and with all the anxiety and happiness this entails. We turn to them, not seeking comfort in the familiarity of the earthly but, above all, in acknowledgment of the unearthly and the extraordinary. We bring our life's experience not in order to find out how we may achieve success, but to see everything in proportion and in a clearer light. We dwell on the scenes before us; we feel them and let our lives merge into them. From the confusion of everyday life, we step into a world whose values lead us to the essential and the eternal.

To those who are overwhelmed by loneliness and despair, the Sorrowful Mysteries have a particular significance. No one is immune to the suffering endemic in the world. Each day brings fresh evidence of personal tragedies or disasters of mind-numbing proportion through the immediacy of the press. We struggle to understand these things in order to make our lives bearable. Such events sharpen our understanding of the agony in the garden, the betrayal of Jesus by his friends, the grief of those he loved, and the dereliction of the cross. There can be few who have not experienced loneliness. The desolation of Christ on the cross is the expression of his love and assurance that when we are most alone, he is surely near us. For those who mourn, the image of Mary standing by her dying Son can only bring the deepest consolation. The closing words of the Hail Mary, quietly repeated, will bring great comfort.

The experience of God's presence has been compared to that rare and overwhelming sense of happiness that can occur when we are caught unaware, however momentary or unexpected the occurrence is that causes us to feel inexpressible happiness. This kind of experience is often described as a fleeting knowledge of God, a brief and tantalizing awareness of that which he has prepared for us and which is beyond our wildest imaginings. The Glorious Mysteries spell out the manner in which this fleeting perception becomes reality. It can be deeply consoling to meditate upon the fact that those who were present and witnessed these events were no less bewildered than are we.

Imperceptibly the emphasis shifts from our own existence to a complete absorption into the meditation. As this occurs, the reality of the image gradually expands and fills the mind. Silence descends as the mind quietly moves forward into a different realm, subject only to the gentle reminder of the repeated Hail Marys. The work of the Holy Spirit invades the heart and the mind, assisted by the prayer of Our Lady, for she "treasured all these words and pondered them in her heart" (Luke 2:19). Through her assistance, we are brought to see and understand them.

CHAPTER 7

The Joyful
Mysteries

FIRST JOYFUL MYSTERY

The Annunciation

*J*n his engraving of the Annunciation, David Jones clearly shows us the order of things. The angel, who is the messenger from heaven, bows in reverence before Our Lady who, in turn, inclines her head in acknowledgment of this great honor. The angel Gabriel kneels before the one who was chosen before time began (Genesis 3:15) to be the mother of God. The angel is placed on the earthly side of the picture and, in the distance, the garden echoes the garden of paradise and the tree of knowledge. Mary is separated from this scene and portrayed in an atmosphere of prayer and calm. The angel carries a lily, the sign of purity, as if to emphasize that the baby being announced will be of Adam, but not of the seed of Adam. The woodcut captures an evocation of the obeisance of heaven and a moment of tantalizing suspense, awaiting the acceptance of Mary.

Behind the angel, the gate, once closed, has been opened and a stream of grace flows through.

> In the sixth month the angel Gabriel was sent by God to a town in Galilee called Nazareth, to a virgin engaged to a man whose name was Joseph, of the house of David. The virgin's name was Mary. And he came to her and said, "Greetings, favored one! The Lord is with you." But she was much perplexed by his words and pondered what sort of greeting this might be. The angel said to her, "Do not be afraid, Mary, for you have found favor with God. And now, you will conceive in your womb and bear a son, and you will name him Jesus. He will be great, and will be called the Son of the Most High, and the Lord God will give to him the throne of his ancestor David. He will reign over the house of Jacob forever, and of

his kingdom there will be no end." Mary said to the angel, "How can this be, since I am a virgin?" The angel said to her, "The Holy Spirit will come upon you, and the power of the Most High will overshadow you; therefore the child to be born will be holy; he will be called Son of God. And now, your relative Elizabeth in her old age has also conceived a son; and this is the sixth month for her who was said to be barren. For nothing will be impossible with God." Then Mary said, "Here am I, the servant of the Lord; let it be with me according to your word." Then the angel departed from her (Luke 1:26–38).

Mary was a young girl of thirteen or fourteen when this event took place. As far as we know, she had been brought up by her parents, traditionally known as Saint Anne and Saint Joachim, under the Jewish law. We know from the words of the angel that she was favored of the Lord, who was with her. No more wonderful description could be given. For this description tells us that she was a creature so pleasing to God that her soul was literally a reflection of divine love.

With her humility came also great prudence, for Our Lady was "perplexed by his words and pondered what sort of greeting this might be." She was calmed by the words of the angel, "Do not be afraid," and that in itself is astonishing. In the sheltered and peaceful tenor of her life, such a cosmic occurrence would be enough to unnerve the sturdiest heart, and the words of the angel which followed were no less alarming. For what followed was the announcement of the most important event in the history of the world since the banishment of Adam and Eve from Paradise. The future of the human race hung in the balance for one tantalizing moment; heaven and earth were held in suspense awaiting Mary's *fiat*, or acceptance.

Mary's trust in God prompted her to inquire of the angel the manner in which this event could take place, "since I am a virgin." One can only speculate on the consequences of the angel's request if Mary accepted it. Our Lady was betrothed to Saint Joseph but not yet married. At that time, it was not unknown for a child to be born to a betrothed couple, and it was possible that such a child should be considered legitimate. If, however, the woman was found to have been unfaithful to her betrothed, death by stoning was the usual punishment. Joseph knew that unfaithfulness on Mary's part was unthinkable, but one can still imagine the depth of his inward crisis.

Like all those brought up in the Jewish faith, Mary's knowledge of the Scriptures was extensive. She must, therefore, have been somehow aware of the terrible suffering that awaited the Messiah, and of her own suffering that would be entailed upon her acceptance.

None of these speculations appears to have clouded her submission or her acceptance of the will of God. And having received Our Lady's words, "let it be with me according to your word," the angel left her without any consoling explanation or comfort. But the future of the human race had been assured.

Prayer

Descend,
Holy Spirit of Life!
Come down into our hearts,
that we may live.
Descend into emptiness,
that emptiness
may be filled.
Descend into the dust,
that the dust may flower.
Descend into the dark,
that the light
may shine in darkness.

Amen.

SECOND JOYFUL MYSTERY

The Visitation

*J*n this picture, Elizabeth as the older woman is seated to receive the greeting of her cousin, and in this way the artist emphasizes the homage that John the Baptist offered even from his mother's womb. John must look up to the child Our Lady carries. Wherever she goes, Mary brings Jesus and, as the halos of the two women merge, it is as if John the Baptist greets his Lord. Zechariah is partly obscured and apart from the scene. He is unable to accept the miracle before him, and his feet are firmly placed in the everyday world. His head, inclined toward the holiness of the room, hints at his dilemma.

> In those days Mary set out and went with haste to a Judean town in the hill country, where she entered the house of Zechariah and greeted Elizabeth. When Elizabeth heard Mary's greeting, the child leaped in her womb. And Elizabeth was filled with the Holy Spirit and exclaimed with a loud cry, "Blessed are you among women, and blessed is the fruit of your womb. And why has this happened to me, that the mother of my Lord comes to me? For as soon as I heard the sound of your greeting, the child in my womb leaped for joy. And blessed is she who believed that there would be a fulfillment of what was spoken to her by the Lord" (Luke 1:39–45).

The journey Mary embarked upon was daunting. In a land that was rife with violence, she undertook the journey on foot, accompanied—according to tradition—by a single female attendant. Having accepted the will of God, Our Lady did not just sit back and await events. Knowing that her cousin was in need of her, she set off without hesitation to be with Elizabeth.

Our Lady brought the child within her to Elizabeth as she will bring him to us if we will turn to her. She need not have feared any lack of understanding on the part of Elizabeth. Inspired by the Holy Spirit, her cousin greets her with the words that echo those of the angel Gabriel, "Blessed are you among women," and the unborn John the Baptist leaps in greeting to his Lord.

The words of the *Magnificat* uttered by Mary in reply to Elizabeth remind us once more of the knowledge of the Old Testament that Mary possessed. Every line in this joyful announcement that God had visited his people is full of allusion to the Bible.

This is the longest utterance recorded of Our Lady, who is normally so sparing of words. It is interesting that on this occasion Mary's humility takes a different form and she is overwhelmed with joy.

> "My soul magnifies the Lord,
> and my spirit rejoices in God my Savior,
> for he has looked with favor on the lowliness of his
> servant.
> Surely, from now on all generations will call me
> blessed;
> for the Mighty One has done great things for me,
> and holy is his name.
> His mercy is for those who fear him
> from generation to generation.
> He has shown strength with his arm;
> he has scattered the proud in the thoughts of
> their hearts.

He has brought down the powerful from their
thrones,
and lifted up the lowly;
he has filled the hungry with good things,
and sent the rich away empty.
He has helped his servant Israel,
in remembrance of his mercy,
according to the promise he made to our ancestors,
to Abraham and to his descendants forever."

(Luke 1:46–55)

Prayer

Breath of Heaven,
carry us on the impulse
of Christ's love,
as easily as thistledown
is carried on the wind;
that in the Advent season of our souls,
while He is formed in us,
in secret and in silence—
the Creator
in the hands of his creatures,
as the Host
in the hands of the priest—
we may carry Him forth
to wherever He wishes to be,
as Mary carried Him over the hills
on His errand of love,
to the house of Elizabeth.

AMEN.

THIRD JOYFUL MYSTERY

The Nativity

Mary and Joseph gaze down in wonder and love at the child who lifts his arms in a gesture of giving. He stretches out his arm as if to foretell his death on the cross. The star glows above the shepherds who crowd in the entrance, and on the right the animals kneel. Above the scene of intimacy and love, the Holy Spirit hovers in the form of a dove.

> While they were there, the time came for her to de- liver her child. And she gave birth to her firstborn son and wrapped him in bands of cloth, and laid him in a manger, because there was no place for them in the inn.
>
> In that region there were shepherds living in the fields, keeping watch over their flock by night. Then an angel of the Lord stood before them, and the glory of the Lord shone around them, and they were terri- fied. But the angel said to them, "Do not be afraid; for see—I am bringing you good news of great joy for all the people: to you is born this day in the city of David a Savior, who is the Messiah, the Lord. This will be a sign for you: you will find a child wrapped in bands of cloth and lying in a manger." And suddenly there was with the angel a multitude of the heavenly host, praising God and saying,
>
> "Glory to God in the highest heaven,
> and on earth peace among those
> whom he favors!" (Luke 2:6–14).

Caesar Augustus was intent on his grandiose plan to take a census of the world. As far as the census-takers of the time were concerned, "the world" meant the Roman Empire. Thus, notices went up everywhere ordering people to return to their town of origin in order to register. Despite the imminence of the birth of the holy child, Joseph felt impelled to set out immediately on the arduous journey from Nazareth to Bethlehem.

Joseph must have felt confident of finding shelter somewhere in his hometown, despite the thronging crowd arriving from all directions in obedience to Caesar's command. As they went from door to door, becoming increasingly tired, it would have become apparent that Roman soldiers and other wealthy visitors had found shelter, but for them there was nothing. That sad line, "There was no place for them at the inn," echoes forlornly in Saint Luke's Gospel. Eventually room—if it could be called that—was found in a stable beneath the inn, among the animals.

It is appropriate that the animals should be present at the birth of God-made-man. Untrammeled by human considerations, they stay quietly by the manger, unaware of the astounding event taking place in their midst, and resting peacefully in the presence of their maker.

Our Lord did not announce himself to the world. Through an angel, his coming was made known to some shepherds, and the Magi were informed by a star. Two completely different sorts of people: the shepherds in their simplicity recognized divinity, and the Magi in their wisdom were not influenced by appearances.

The shepherds came immediately and did not find the poverty strange; they probably knew that King David had himself been a shepherd. Seeing the connection, the words of the angel had filled them with joy. The Magi were slightly more cautious, as the clever have a tendency to be. They took the precaution of verifying the direction of the star at the court of King Herod—a fatal diversion.

To Herod the news was grim indeed. He feared the end of his reign with the coming of the Messianic King of the Jews. He sought to forestall the will of God by striking out violently against the innocent—the reaction of tyrants throughout history.

We wince in pity at the massacre of the innocents, which is repeated to this day in abortion clinics, in famine, and in wars around the world. The birth of the holy child proclaims the sanctity of life and, at the same time, underscores the vulnerability of innocence that must rely totally on the protective care and love of parents.

The old Roman word for charity, *caritas*, meant love of family or close relations; interested love rather than disinterested. After Bethlehem, charity was transformed by the love of the holy child into love for the entire human race. We see its fruits today when people separated by thousands of miles can be moved to loving pity and practical aid for others who are starving or suffering; in the work of Mother Teresa for the poor, and in the work of hospices throughout the world where the dying are cared for with love. Such disinterested love flows from the stable at Bethlehem.

Humility, too, has taken on a new meaning apart from the old understanding of "lowness" or "meanness." Not the false modesty dictated by so-called good manners which obliges people to deny their God-given gifts, nor an obsequious fawning before superiors, but the humility of those people who silently and happily place others before themselves, who accept injustice without rancor. That is the humility that arose out of Bethlehem where the Son of God was born in a stable.

Prayer

Be born in us,
Incarnate Love.
Take our flesh and blood,
and give us Your humanity;
take our eyes, and give us Your vision;
take our minds,
and give us Your pure thought;
take our feet and set them in Your path;
take our hands
and fold them in Your prayer;
take our hearts
and give them Your will to love.

AMEN.

FOURTH JOYFUL MYSTERY

The Presentation

*J*n this portrayal, Mary bends over her child with anxious tenderness as she presents him to Simeon, who in turn looks heavenward as he kneels in the knowledge that this is the miracle he has been awaiting with such confidence. Anna stands holding the Scriptures that foretell the birth of a savior while Saint Joseph, holding the two turtledoves, seems consumed with concern for Mary and her child.

> When the time came for their purification according to the law of Moses, they brought him up to Jerusalem to present him to the Lord (as it is written in the law of the Lord, "Every firstborn male shall be designated as holy to the Lord"), and they offered a sacrifice according to what is stated in the law of the Lord, "a pair of turtledoves or two young pigeons" (Luke 2:22–24).

Under the Law of Moses, a mother was considered unclean after the birth of a child. So Mary had to present herself at the Temple to be purified, at the same time presenting her firstborn son. Despite the fact that Mary was the mother of God, there was no exemption for her, nor in her humility did she ever seek to do other than follow the law in obedience.

The usual offering was a lamb, but owing to the extreme poverty of Our Lady and Saint Joseph, they were permitted to offer two turtledoves. We are told about that holy pair, Simeon and Anna, who were present in the Temple. Simeon had waited and prayed in the Temple throughout his long life and immediately recognized in the Holy Child, the Redeemer he had awaited for so many years. Inspired by the Holy Spirit, he uttered the words of the *Nunc Dimittis*:

"Master, now you are dismissing your
servant in peace,
according to your word;
for my eyes have seen your salvation,
which you have prepared in the presence
of all peoples,
a light for revelation to the Gentiles
and for glory to your people Israel."

(Luke 2:29–32)

How patiently he had waited, and how wonderfully that patience was rewarded. Anna, too, had waited many lonely years for that same joy, and her patience was also rewarded.

As for Our Lady, she was told that a sword of sorrow would pierce her heart, but she must have already feared this. We are protected from knowledge of the future, but for Our Lady her suffering was spelled out unmercifully even while she held the baby in her arms.

Prayer

By the humility
of Jesus, Mary and Joseph
give us the glory of humility.
By the mystery
of innocence
obeying the law
binding upon sinners,
make us obedient.
By the offering of the poor,
the two white doves
in the gentle hands
of the pure Mother of Love,
give us the spirit of poverty.

AMEN.

The Finding
in the Temple

ary greets Jesus with joy and, although he returns her embrace, his hands and the inclination of his body remain in a gesture of instruction to the row of solemn men of learning before him. We only see half the face of Saint Joseph, which is turned to Mary with concern. We see his pleasure at the reunion of Mary with her son, but apart from this he has little understanding of the scene before him.

> And when he was twelve years old, they went up as usual for the festival. When the festival was ended and they started to return, the boy Jesus stayed behind in Jerusalem, but his parents did not know it. Assuming that he was in the group of travelers, they went a day's journey. Then they started to look for him among their relatives and friends. When they did not find him, they returned to Jerusalem to search for him. After three days they found him in the temple, sitting among the teachers, listening to them and asking them questions. And all who heard him were amazed at his understanding and his answers. When his parents saw him they were astonished; and his mother said to him, "Child, why have you treated us like this? Look, your father and I have been searching for you with great anxiety." He said to them, "Why were you searching for me? Did you not know that I must be in my Father's house?" But they did not understand what he had said to them (Luke 2:42–50).

The holy family responds to the dictates of the Law which requires that all men should attend the three great feasts of the Passover, Pentecost, and Tabernacles. On reaching the age of twelve, Jesus was considered mature in the eyes of the law, and therefore was able to join his parents for the first time.

The loss of Our Lord for three days is one of the seven sorrows of Our Lady. Not only did she suffer as any mother who loses a child, but in her heart she also knew that her son would eventually be put to death by his own people. Since Jesus had now reached maturity, she must have wondered if the time of his death was upon them. Mary suffered the dark night of all who lose God, and she was to suffer again for the three days between the Crucifixion and the Resurrection.

In a sermon on the finding in the Temple, the twelfth-century abbot Aelred of Rievaulx pointed out that Our Lord often withdraws himself for a short time in order to make us search more diligently for him. The mystery of the finding in the Temple, therefore, is the image of the quest of the devout soul.

Apart from being relieved, Mary and Joseph must have been amazed to find Jesus among the pupils in the school of rabbis and seated before the learned priests and scribes: this child of twelve sitting calmly before the elders. The minds of the rabbis and scribes are befuddled with layers of legislative knowledge, yet they listen attentively to the wisdom of their Lord and God. Saint Luke, with great economy of words, says simply that they were "amazed."

This mystery is firmly placed among the joys despite the contrast between the words of Jesus in the Temple when he teaches us that the things of God must come before all things in this world that we love the most, and the calm serenity of the image of life within the holy family evoked by Saint Luke at the end of this story.

Then he went down with them and came to Nazareth, and was obedient to them. His mother treasured all these things in her heart.

And Jesus increased in wisdom and in years, and in divine and human favor (Luke 2:51–52).

Prayer

Through Mary,
seeking her lost son,
may we be given grace
always to seek for the Christ Child
and always to find Him.
Let us find Him in all children,
and in all who have a child's needs—
the helpless, the sick, the simple,
the aged;
in all who serve
and are trusting and poor;
in all who are lonely or homeless.
Let us too become as little children,
to find the Divine Child
in our own hearts.

AMEN.

CHAPTER 8

The Sorrowful Mysteries

FIRST SORROWFUL MYSTERY

The Agony in the Garden

*J*esus kneels among the olive trees, arms outstretched in prayer, and his loneliness is accentuated by the sleeping disciples. The whole scene is bathed in eerie moonlight. Again the gate is portrayed, this time slightly ajar, as a reminder that redemption can only be completed by Jesus leaving the garden and enduring the suffering on the cross. From the direction of the city walls in the distance, we can almost hear the rhythmic marching of the approaching mob whose faces are concealed by hoods, a strangely contemporary note. The river runs through the woodcut, depicted almost as a torrent as if to underline the impending violence.

> After Jesus had spoken these words, he went out with his disciples across the Kidron valley to a place where there was a garden, which he and his disciples entered (John 18:1).

As if to underline the rocky nature of the countryside, Saint Luke describes Our Lord withdrawing from the others a "stone's throw" away. The rocks must have cast foreboding shadows across the hill, the twisted limbs of the olive trees standing eerily on the skyline like some distended cross, announcing the gathering forces of evil to an already bleak scene. The sounds of the assembling mob in the distance, the shouts and the cracking of sticks being torn from the ground, all carried on the still night air to the place where Jesus knelt.

Even in his hour of desolation, Jesus still teaches us with loving awareness of our weakness. To what immense lengths we will go to avoid suffering; whole industries are involved in producing panaceas for every ill. Any suffering is believed to be a grievous injustice: it is the "right" of every person to be free from all discomfort. In contrast, to the saints, suffering became the very means of salvation.

Our Lord prayed until his sweat turned to drops of blood. Because of his divinity, Christ knew precisely what was to befall him during the hours of excruciating torture that lay ahead, and even more serious was the knowledge of the sin that would continue to be committed and remain unrepented until the end of time. He prayed, "My Father, if this cannot pass away unless I drink it, your will be done" (Matthew 26:42).

We are told of the angel who was sent to comfort Our Lord, and this visit from above adds another aspect to be pondered over in this desolate scene. Our Lord had turned for comfort to the three disciples: Peter, the rock on which he would found his Church; John, the beloved; and his brother, James—and they responded by falling asleep. The New Testament has several warnings to us to remain spiritually alert; and above all the words of Jesus to the three disciples: "Keep awake and pray that you may not come into the time of trial; the spirit indeed is willing, but the flesh is weak" (Mark 14:38). Eventually their drowsy watch is brought to an abrupt halt as the din of the approaching mob grows louder, and they go forward to meet the crowd.

Prayer

By your heaviness and fear
in Gethsemane,
comfort the oppressed
and those who are afraid.
By Your loneliness,
facing the Passion
while the Apostles slept,
comfort those who face evil alone
while the world sleeps.
By Your persistent prayer,
in anguish of anticipation,
strengthen those
who shrink from the unknown.
By Your humility,
taking the comfort of angels,
give us grace to help
and to be helped by one another,
and in one another
to comfort You, Jesus Christ.

Amen.

SECOND SORROWFUL MYSTERY

*The Scourging
at the Pillar*

*J*esus is tied to the pillar, his arms extended above his head in order that the pain inflicted may be all the more severe. Two soldiers are chosen to inflict the stripes, their muscles extended by their exertions. The soldiers witnessing the scene display a curiosity and fascination unmarked by any pity.

> So after they had gathered, Pilate said to them, "Whom do you want me to release for you, Jesus Barabbas or Jesus who is called the Messiah?" For he realized that it was out of jealousy that they had handed him over. While he was sitting on the judgment seat, his wife sent word to him, "Have nothing to do with that innocent man, for today I have suffered a great deal because of a dream about him." Now the chief priests and the elders persuaded the crowds to ask for Barabbas and to have Jesus killed. The governor again said to them, "Which of the two do you want me to release for you?" And they said, "Barabbas." Pilate said to them, "Then what should I do with Jesus who is called the Messiah?" All of them said, "Let him be crucified!" (Matthew 27:17–22).

And along they all come, egging one another on with shouts and waving arms until, anticlimactically, they come to a clattering halt in front of Jesus. Lost for the moment, they seem unable to decide on their next move, standing there rather stupidly; Saint John tells us that Judas stood with them. And when Jesus quietly inquires of this sea of faces, "Who do you seek?" and replies to their demand, "I am he," they stumble backward, falling over one another.

For one precious second, the voice of innocence silences evil, but the betrayal of Judas ensures that the crowd, now even more enraged by shame, grab Jesus and, to justify their fury, bind his hands with rope. Such is the power of innocence that this huge mob felt safe only when Our Lord, alone and defenseless, was tightly bound. For now we know the blunt truth, which is that the disciples had abandoned Jesus and run away into the night. Saint John tells us that Jesus was first led to Annas, before being taken on to his son-in-law, Caiaphas, the high priest. And there, the priests, elders, and scribes look for some means of condemning Jesus.

There was no shortage of people rushing forward to invent accusations, but even in these extraordinary circumstances, the evidence was ludicrous. Eventually, the high priest rose to his feet, subduing the rabble to ask Jesus if he was indeed "the Christ, the Son of God," to which he replied, "You have said it." Triumphant that he might at last have a case, the high priest, like any tyrant, turns to his cowed followers for approval. But another problem now looms for the mob: their law forbade them to put a man to death; they could go no further than the reply that Jesus was "guilty of death." Someone else must be found to carry out that sentence, and they knew that Pontius Pilate was their man.

Pilate is mystified at first by the babbling of vague accusations, "We found this man perverting our nation, forbidding us to pay taxes to the emperor." In Saint John's account, the chief priests appear even more uneasy, unable to find anything more convincing than "if he were not a criminal, we would not have handed him over to you." But Pilate grasps the reason for their envy and hatred: they are saying that Jesus has proclaimed himself their King. Pilate now understands the situation, as far as he is able, and knows what the Jewish leaders require of him. He is in an agony of indecision. When he hears the words of Jesus, "Everyone who belongs to the truth listens to my voice," he replies wearily, "What is truth?" and he returns to the crowd saying, "I find no case against him."

Pilate then offers to release one prisoner to them as was the custom on the feast of Passover. They take up his offer and choose Barabbas and, amid shouts of "crucify him" when he suggests Jesus be released instead, Pilate capitulates to the rule of the mob. How blind we are in our efforts to save our skin in the eyes of the world; but Pilate has one last, desperate card to play. In sending Our Lord to be scourged, he clung to the hope that the bloodlust of Jesus' enemies might thus be satisfied and they would be shamed into releasing him. This was the greatest cruelty. Scourging was often inflicted on the condemned man before crucifixion. It was inflicted by several soldiers with metal-tipped leather thongs and continued until a state of excruciating physical agony was achieved, but it stopped short of death in order to ensure that the victim could still suffer on the cross.

Prayer

Lord,
Mocked
and scourged at the pillar,
when Pilate made his pitiful effort
to compromise,
by scourging Innocence.
Christ, so gentle
to the weakness and folly of men,
make us patient
with the lash and whip of circumstance,
with the bruising of life,
the thong for our own shoulders,
made by our own weakness,
malice and stupidity;
help us to accept it
as our just due,
not complaining,
but with the dignity
and humility
of Your imperious will.

AMEN.

THIRD SORROWFUL MYSTERY

The Crowning
with Thorns

T he soldiers now crowd around Jesus in their effort to mock and ridicule the figure before them. They even make crude obeisance before him, laughing at his pain. He sits in dignity, his head bowed in compassion and forgiveness and his hand raised in blessing, for "they do not know what they are doing."

> And they clothed him in a purple cloak; and after twisting some thorns into a crown, they put it on him. And they began saluting him, "Hail, King of the Jews!" They struck his head with a reed, spat upon him, and knelt down in homage to him (Mark 15:17–19).

Here, if ever it was needed, is the evidence that things are rarely as they appear. This sad and bleeding figure is the savior of the world. Earthly kings and leaders are usually surrounded by pomp and circumstance and, in modern times, with layers of security, and yet this pathetic figure was the Son of God, the King of all kings, the Creator of the world, that now mocks him and spits upon him. The sin of humankind gives vent to terrible vengeance, and Jesus freely accepts torture and death for our sins. His love for his creation is beyond all human comprehension.

The irony of the situation is intentional. One of the principal reasons for the hatred of the chief priests was Our Lord's claim to be the King of the Jews. They were well aware that a final, Messianic age had been foretold in the prophecies of the Old Testament, and now these prophecies were being strongly and painfully fulfilled. For the soldiers, who had so cruelly beaten the prisoner, no biblical predictions clouded their minds. They merely looked upon such claimants to kingship and divinity—and there were several—as tiresome troublemakers causing civil disturbance and putting more work on the military.

And now, with all the energy of bullies let loose upon the innocent, the soldiers set about Jesus, crushing a circlet of thorns into his forehead. Seeing the blood pouring down his face onto the cloak, which was already clinging to his open wounds, their sarcasm knows no bounds. They kneel before Jesus, sneering in mock obeisance. Having handed him the "scepter" of weakness, a reed, they snatch it from him and start to drive the thorns more deeply into his brow as they strike his head and face.

And then it appears that Pilate, the man, separates himself from Pilate, the governor, and is alone before his Creator. With almost childlike curiosity, Pilate asks Jesus where he comes from. He is made even more uneasy by Jesus' silence. Pilate reminds him that he, as governor, has the power to crucify him or set him free. Our Lord replies, "You would have no power over me unless it had been given you from above; therefore the one who handed me over to you is guilty of a greater sin" (John 19:11). In that moment of truth, with the eyes of Our Lord upon him, Pilate seeks to escape the dreadful predicament in which he finds himself. But the roar of the crowd overwhelms him, and the punishment that Caesar would inflict on him for misrule seems more real than the injustice he is about to mete out on Christ. Pilate succumbs.

In one final futile jibe at the crowd, Pilate asks them if he should crucify their king. In a deafening shout, the chief priests reject the kingship of Christ, and Jesus is led away.

Prayer

Christ, crowned with thorns,
give us courage to think,
to sift and measure and weigh;
to wrestle with the angel,
and if need be,
to enter into darkness,
disillusion and doubt,
in the search for truth.
Illumine our minds,
though our eyes be blinded
by Your bright ray.
Crown us, Your servants,
with the only crown fitting
for vassals of the Lord of Light:
crown us, Lord,
with Your crown
of thorns.

AMEN.

The Carrying
of the Cross

*J*esus bows down beneath the weight of the cross. The soldiers wielding sticks goad him and one is even leaning on the cross to increase its already dreadful weight. The grieving women, their hands joined in prayer, lean tenderly toward him as he passes by.

> Then he handed him over to them to be crucified. So they took Jesus; and carrying the cross by himself, he went out to what is called The Place of the Skull, which in Hebrew is called Golgotha (John 19:16–17).

Within the space of one week, something had changed the peaceful, rejoicing crowd of Palm Sunday, with their joyful chant of "Hosanna" into the vengeful mob with its roar of "Crucify him."

To all intents and purposes, this mob decision appeared to be a democratic one; the choice of the people to bludgeon vacillating authority at the cost of the innocent. Propaganda and public opinion (which often means nothing of the sort) had been at work. The chief priests and their followers, aware that their grip on events was threatened, moved into action. Their emissaries may well have gone from house to house spreading deceit and inciting hatred.

Some of those who had hailed Jesus only a week before were perhaps among those who now disowned him as he was led beyond the city walls to the place of crucifixion.

The procession is made up of officials, the centurion with his detachment of soldiers, the two thieves, and Our Lord. They make their way through the crowd, silent at last apart from the few jeers still to be heard from stragglers hurrying to catch up, fearful of missing a moment of the drama.

The cross was roughly thrust onto the torn and bleeding shoulders of Christ. Splinters would have pressed into his shoulder as he moved forward under its great weight. Isaiah had foretold that "authority rests upon his shoulder" (Isaiah 9:5), and Our Lord himself had said, "Whoever does not take up the cross and follow me is not worthy of me" (Matthew 10:38). And again, "If any want to become my followers, let them deny themselves and take up their cross and follow me. For those who want to save their life will lose it, and those who lose their life for my sake will find it" (Matthew 16:24–25). The way of the cross demonstrates to us that the path to heaven is made up of one small step at a time in patience and self-denial, following the example of the road to Calvary.

The soldiers were fearful that if Jesus fell yet again under the weight of the cross he might die before reaching Calvary. They looked around for someone to carry the cross, because this task was too demeaning for a Roman soldier. Their eyes fell on a visitor among the crowd, one Simon of Cyrene, unknown until now, but to be remembered for all time for this one brief moment. Simon was probably unwilling to be pulled into the drama but rose to the occasion and took up his burden. Some who have suffering thrust upon them accept it with resignation and even joy, as the means of salvation. Simon of Cyrene must have been such a one, for Saint Mark's Gospel implies that this man's sons, Alexander and Rufus, no doubt influenced by the action of their father, became Christians (Mark 15:21).

Simon was not the only one in that hostile crowd to be moved with pity for Our Lord, although most of his disciples and friends seem to have vanished with undignified haste. Women do not appear to have been among those who called for his blood: "His blood be on us and on our children" (Matthew 27:25). The only woman who makes an appearance during the trial is the wife of Pilate, who so urgently begged him to have nothing to do with Our Lord (Matthew 27:19).

Legend describes Veronica bravely making her way through the crowd to wipe the dirt and blood from the face of Jesus with a linen cloth. Her love must have been brave and certain to enable her to courageously elbow her way through that angry mob, probably pushing, shoving, and jeering at her.

And the women of Jerusalem weep in pity. Jesus stops and breaks his silence. At a time when he might have been overwhelmed with grief and suffering, he speaks words of comfort and concern for them.

> "Daughters of Jerusalem, do not weep for me, but weep for yourselves and for your children. For, as the days are surely coming when they will say, 'Blessed are the barren and the wombs that never bore, and the breasts that never nursed.' Then they will begin to say to the mountains, 'Fall on us'; and to the hills, 'Cover us.' For if they do this when the wood is green, what will happen when it is dry?" (Luke 23:28–31).

Jesus was the "green wood," the tree of life; the "dry wood" was the doomed city of Jerusalem, and later the world which would be deaf to his word. Having spoken these words, he went on his way until the hill of Calvary was reached.

Prayer

Lord,
Let us take up the cross;
it is the heavy load of our sins—
our pride and materialism and greed.
We all share the responsibility
of lifting it from the backs
of the innocents
who are crushed under it.
Let our Communion with You,
and with one another,
be proved by our will to suffer.
So that all our hands,
lifting the bitter wood together,
may lighten it for each other
and each of us
may be a Cyrenian to You,
Christ, through the ages
bearing our cross.

AMEN.

FIFTH SORROWFUL MYSTERY

The Crucifixion

*J*esus hangs on the cross. "Sweet Christ's dear Tree," are David Jones's own words. His mother, Mary, and Saint John stand beneath him, mute in their grief, while Mary Magdalene embraces his dying body. Jesus turns to the Good Thief, who turns his face trustingly toward him, while the bad thief hangs his head in bitterness. The motionless figure of the centurion is strangely moving, for we know that he watches the scene with a growing awareness of the significance of the figure before him.

> It was now about noon, and darkness came over the whole land until three in the afternoon, while the sun's light failed; and the curtain of the temple was torn in two. Then Jesus, crying with a loud voice, said, "Father, into your hands I commend my spirit." Having said this, he breathed his last. When the centurion saw what had taken place, he praised God and said, "Certainly this man was innocent" (Luke 23:44–47).

Death ultimately means the punishment of sin. Until the sin of Adam, death had no place in God's plan. Until the sting of death was drawn by Jesus, there was no hope for humankind. As Jesus arrived at Calvary, the gruesome act of sacrifice entered its final stage.

Having roughly torn the clothes from the body of Christ, the soldiers prepare to nail his hands and feet to the cross. The precise positioning of the nails was a carefully calculated means of inflicting the greatest pain, while at the same time ensuring that the hands were not actually torn from the wrists. The soldiers' fearful work was done. The last hammer blow echoes around the city walls below, and the cross is lifted and placed in the pit prepared for it. The extended, pinioned arms of Jesus take his full weight as he hangs before the soldiers, who are now exhausted by their task.

Those who were crucified would sometimes, in their excruciating pain, shout down foul abuse on those who passed by. In his agony, Our Lord's concern was for his persecutors: "Father, forgive them; for they do not know not what they are doing." Any human tragedy will always attract the curious, and while the scene of the crucifixion unfolds, the people remain, staring in fascination. They "stood at a distance and watched these things," says Saint Matthew; the other evangelists make the same calm yet reproachful observation.

Egged on by the rapt attention of the crowd, the chief priests and onlookers taunt Jesus, urging him to prove he is Israel's king and God's Son by coming down from the cross and saving himself (Matthew 27:39–44). Jesus could certainly have accepted their challenge and come down from the cross, fully restored to healthy manhood. But all that took place had in fact been foretold: Jesus came down to earth in order to take all humanity to paradise. His sacrifice for the salvation of all of us had been anticipated from the time of the Fall. In the bleak garden of Calvary, Redemption was achieved.

On either side of Jesus were crucified the two thieves. The first one, like many criminals before and after, cursed his fate and swore at the onlookers, although his punishment, horrific as it was, was in accordance with theLaw of the time. The second thief understood this but said to Jesus, "Jesus, remember me when you come into your kingdom." And Jesus replied, "Truly I tell you, today you will be with me in Paradise" (Luke 23:42–43). How strange to think that the first person to follow Our Lord into Paradise was a condemned thief who was the first to receive the fruits of Calvary. The centurion who had supervised the crucifixion also made his confession of faith at Calvary and would enter Paradise.

After three hours of agony, Our Lord was close to death. Silhouetted against a darkening sky were the figures of John, Christ's beloved disciple, and Mary, his mother, standing bowed in grief at the foot of the cross. What must have been their thoughts? The other disciples had fled and were hiding in the shadows of the city. Only Saint John, Our Lady, and some other women remained. They cannot have fully understood what was happening. They saw only that their beloved was hanging, bleeding, and dying, before them. Mary had known from the beginning that a sword would pierce her heart, but no warning could have prepared her for this. In the gathering gloom, they heard the voice of Jesus coming down to them deep and true, unbroken by pain. "When Jesus saw his mother and the disciple whom he loved standing beside her, he said to his mother, 'Woman, here is your son.' Then he said to the disciple, 'Here is your mother.' And from that hour the disciple took her into his own home" (John 19:26–27). By addressing his mother as "woman," Jesus was reminding us of the words of Genesis 3:15, "I will put enmity between you and the woman, / and between your offspring and hers; / he will strike your head, / and you will strike his heel." She was that woman, and he was her seed. Only through her *fiat*, or acceptance of the angel's message, was God's plan carried out. As she was there in the beginning of the redemptive drama, she was there, too, at the final scene.

How can we ignore his dying request to Saint John that his grieving mother should be honored? And Jesus made us the astonishing gift of Mary as our heavenly mother, in his words to Saint John, "Here is your mother." Who could carry our imperfect prayers more perfectly to her Son than Mary? The prayer of the rosary brings us ever closer to Calvary, to stand silently by those two figures at the foot of the cross.

Then he bowed his head and gave up his spirit.
(John 19:30)

Prayer

Nail our hands
in Your hands
to the Cross.
Make us take and hold
the hard thing.
Nail our feet,
in Your feet
to the Cross,
that they may never
wander away from You.
Make our promises and our vows,
nails that hold us fast,
that even our dead weight of sin,
dragging on the nails
in our last weakness,
may not separate us from You,
but may make us one with You
in Your redeeming love.

AMEN.

CHAPTER 9

The Glorious Mysteries

FIRST GLORIOUS MYSTERY

The Resurrection

*T*he stone is rolled away from the dark and cavernous tomb, the stream of grace is flowing from it. In the midst of a garden of flowers and olive trees, Jesus is risen again. His head is inclined in gentle reassurance to Mary Magdalene; his hands, marked by the nails, are raised in blessing. Mary kneels, her face raised in happiness, as she greets her Lord.

> When the sabbath was over, Mary Magdalene, and Mary the mother of James, and Salome bought spices, so that they might go and anoint him. And very early on the first day of the week, when the sun had risen, they went to the tomb. They had been saying to one another, "Who will roll away the stone for us from the entrance to the tomb?" When they looked up, they saw that the stone, which was very large, had already been rolled back. As they entered the tomb, they saw a young man, dressed in a white robe, sitting on the right side; and they were alarmed. But he said to them, "Do not be alarmed; you are looking for Jesus of Nazareth, who was crucified. He has been raised; he is not here. Look, there is the place they laid him. But go, tell his disciples and Peter that he is going ahead of you to Galilee; there you will see him, just as he told you" (Mark 16:1–7).

The secret friends of Jesus, those who had visited him at night, now take their honored place in history. Joseph of Arimathea had been to see Pilate to ask for the body of Christ and, together with Nicodemus and a few devoted followers, they prepared to take Our Lord down from the cross. Mary must have been present as Christ's devoted friends carefully

lifted the torn limbs from the grip of the nails and removed
the thorns from his brow, before they placed him in her arms.
How different were the thoughts of the woman who now, in
anguish, held the broken body of her son from those feelings
of the young mother who had smiled down on her child so
many years before. They anointed the body with myrrh and
spices and wrapped it carefully in white linen. Saint John says,
"Now there was a garden in the place where he was crucified,
and in the garden there was a new tomb in which no one had
ever been laid" (John 19:41). And there they laid him, rolling
a large stone across the entrance before these friends vanished
into the night and into obscurity.

What can have been the thoughts of the disciples? They
had fled from the scene before the trial of Our Lord and nothing had been heard of them since. They were cowering in fear,
heartbroken at the turn of events and, in their panic, completely forgetting that on many occasions they had been warned
of what lay ahead. How often we doubt the promises of Christ.
Apart from anything else, we feel that we are not up to much
and certainly do not merit the future he holds out to us, so we
turn away. While no one can ever "deserve" redemption, we
reject salvation if we fail to take literally the words of Christ.
He had told the disciples that he would rise again on the third
day, but none of them believed it.

Ironically, it appears that the only ones to place any faith
in Christ's words were the chief priests and the pharisees,
and they hurriedly dispatched soldiers to mount guard on
the tomb (Matthew 27:62–64). They even set a time limit of
three days for the guard duty, revealing their fear of the words
of Christ, "I will destroy this temple made with hands, and
in three days I will build another, not made with hands" (Mark
14:58). In some confused way they believed that only the

theft of the body by the disciples could enable this promise to be fulfilled.

At dawn on the morning after the Sabbath, Mary Magdalene, Mary the mother of James, and Salome came to the tomb to embalm the body and to seek consolation in their grief. To their astonishment, the stone was now rolled away and an angel was seated inside the tomb and was saying "Be not frightened," just as the angel had said at the Annunciation. The angel told them the astounding news that Jesus was risen, and was on his way to Galilee, and, with that wonderful concern of heaven for the faint- but loving-hearted, he added, "Go, tell his disciples and Peter that he is going ahead of you to Galilee; there you will see him, just as he told you."

And still the disciples cannot believe it. "But these words seemed to them an idle tale, and they did not believe them" (Luke 24:11). And still later, two other disciples of Jesus walk to Emmaus and are so preoccupied with their grief that they fail to recognize the figure who falls into step beside them. In reply to his gentle questioning, they become voluble and chatter on about the depth of their misery, incapable of hearing or understanding the long list of prophecies foretelling all that had taken place and with which the stranger rebukes them. It is only when Our Lord breaks bread with them that we are told: "Then their eyes were opened, and they recognized him." Saint Thomas, one of the Twelve, even needed to plunge his fingers into the wounded hands before he could accept the risen Christ.

It is perhaps a small consolation to our wavering faith that even those who knew Jesus failed to believe him. But if they had believed more readily, perhaps we would have found it more difficult. "Their infirmity," says Saint Gregory, "was, if I may so put it, our future firmness."

The whole argument of faith rests on this mystery of the Resurrection. Saint Paul says that if it is not a fact that Christ rose from the dead, then our faith is in vain (1 Corinthians 15:14). The feast of Easter is the greatest feast of the Church's year; and, as the Easter candle springs into life, we celebrate a rebirth and promise of resurrection for each and every one in his creation.

For "he was raised on the third day in accordance with the scriptures" (1 Corinthians 15:4).

Prayer

Seed of Eternal life,
sown by love's flowering
in the heavy clay of our hearts,
rise in us;
be our soul's spring.
By the risen feet of Christ,
walking upon the delicate grass;
by the wakened hands of Christ,
touching the cool petals of flowers;
by the opened eyes of Christ,
looking with joy
on all created things;
teach us to wonder,
and to walk upon the earth
aware of earth's loveliness,
aware of the Being of God
in all that is.

Amen.

SECOND GLORIOUS MYSTERY

The Ascension

With Mary in their midst, the eleven apostles watch with uplifted faces as Jesus rises up into heaven. In his hand, Peter holds the keys to the kingdom of heaven.

> While he was blessing them, he withdrew from them
> and was carried up into heaven (Luke 24:51).

The mystery of the Ascension always seems to carry an air of sadness. The disciples had only just begun to understand the reality of the Resurrection, and their joy at the presence of Jesus in their midst must have been overwhelming. And yet he was to leave them once more. Again, they had been warned, and were at least consistent in once more failing to understand the words Our Lord spoke to them. They were happy to be with him and how achingly sad they must have felt when before their eyes, while he blessed them, he departed from them and was carried up into heaven.

When Luke tells the story of the Ascension again in the book of the Acts of the Apostles, he describes the disciples gaping in such astonishment that the angels say, "Men of Galilee, why do you stand looking up toward heaven? This Jesus, who has been taken up from you into heaven, will come in the same way as you saw him go into heaven" (1:11). And then they must have come to their senses, for the Gospel of Luke continues, "And they worshiped him, and returned to Jerusalem with great joy" (24:52). Why should they be so full of joy on this occasion when only forty days before they had run for cover when Our Lord was taken from them for the first time? Something tremendous had happened in those forty days. Christ's Resurrection had transformed their lives.

"Go and tell Peter," the angel at the sepulcher had told the three women (Mark 16:7). Go tell that same Peter who some three days earlier had denied any knowledge of Jesus; that Peter who had run all the way to the sepulcher (John 20:3–10) unable to believe or understand the words of Mary Magdalene, hardly daring to hope as he stared at the empty shroud—dear, marvelous, impetuous Saint Peter who was so astonished to see Our Lord when he appeared by the lake at Galilee that he promptly jumped out of the boat in his joy. And when he had finally recovered himself and Our Lord asked him if he loved him, Saint Peter was mystified that he should even ask. His love was unwavering when Jesus had asked him who people said he was. On that occasion Our Lord had said, "You are Peter and on this rock I will build my church. And the gates of hell will not prevail against it."

Saint Peter seems to have made a muddle of most things after that—trying to dissuade Jesus from the cross, because he loved him, falling asleep when Our Lord asked him to watch with him in the Garden of Olives, and denying him three times on the night of his trial. And yet the angel was quite specific that it was Peter who was to be told that Jesus had risen.

The risen Lord had first appeared to a woman who had had seven demons driven from her (Luke 8:2), and then to Peter who had denied him—both of them sinners who had repented. We have only to think of that look Our Lord gave Saint Peter after his third denial to realize how bitterly Saint Peter had wept. Upon that rock the Church was indeed founded; and Peter was to die the same death as his Lord, only legend has it that he insisted he was unworthy of such honor, and was crucified upside down.

> And Jesus came and said to them, "All authority in heaven and on earth has been given to me. Go therefore and make disciples of all nations, baptizing them

in the name of the Father and of the Son and of the Holy Spirit, and teaching them to obey everything that I have commanded you. And remember, I am with you always, to the end of the age" (Matthew 28:18–20).

Prayer

Christ,
Ascended into heaven,
You bear the wounds of the whole world
in Your hands and feet and in Your heart.
They plead for us,
shining like stars
before the secret face of God.
By Your five wounds
purify our five senses;
lift up our hearts into heaven.
While You draw down
God's mercy to us,
showing our wounds
in Your glorified Body,
let us draw men up to You,
showing Your wounds to the world,
scored on our grey dust
in the bright crimson of Your love.

AMEN.

The Descent
of the Holy Spirit

.

T he apostles are gathered in the upper room with Mary in their midst. The Holy Spirit descends with shafts of light. Gone is the paradise garden to be replaced by the world in which the apostles will spread the word.

> When the day of Pentecost had come, they were all together in one place. And suddenly from heaven there came a sound like the rush of a violent wind, and it filled the entire house where they were sitting. Divided tongues, as of fire, appeared among them, and a tongue rested on each of them. All of them were filled with the Holy Spirit and began to speak in other languages, as the Spirit gave them ability (Acts 2:1–4).

From the moment of the Resurrection, Jesus was preparing the disciples for the work that lay ahead, first calming their fears and their disbelief, and then teaching them as their awakening understanding transformed them beyond recognition. "Then he opened their minds to understand the scriptures" (Luke 24:45).

The city of Jerusalem was thronged with crowds drawn by the harvest festival at the time when the disciples, with Mary and the holy women, gathered together in prayer to await the promised coming of the Holy Spirit.

The effect of Pentecost must have been astonishing. A wind suddenly arose around the building, and the crowds gathered in Jerusalem came running from all directions to see light in the form of flames hovering over the heads of the disciples. Even more astonishing was the ease with which the disciples then spoke to each and every person in his or her own language, for the crowds had come from many different areas. At first the crowd accused them of being drunk, but Peter rose to rebuke them. There was no uncertainty about him now, and there was no hesitation as he spoke. When the crowd had heard him out, those same people who had sneered at the disciples only minutes before, became the first fruits of the Holy Spirit. "What shall we do?" they asked Peter, and he preached penance to them and baptized, we are told, about three thousand souls.

Through his special gifts, the Holy Spirit inspires and guides the Church and all its members, if we will allow him to do so. No one person can change the will of another; we may be influenced and cajoled but never forcibly changed. The millions spent on the so-called hidden persuasion of advertising, and the mysterious workings of the psychiatric wards, are a measure of the effort required to attempt the impossible. God alone can change our wills through the workings of the Holy Spirit, who abides in the soul from the moment of baptism, unless we forcibly eject him through sin. Sometimes it seems that we achieve only one small step at a time, before darkness engulfs us. But the gifts of the Holy Spirit are always there for the asking, and give us a true sense of proportion.

Prayer

Come down upon us,
spirit of God,
spirit of wisdom
and peace and joy;
come as a great wind blowing;
sweep our minds with a storm of light.
Be in us as bright fire burning;
forge our wills to shining swords
in the flame.
Purify our hearts
in the crucible
of the fire of love.
Change our tepid nature
into the warm humanity of Christ,
as He changed water to wine.
Be in us a stream of life,
as wine in the living vine.

AMEN.

FOURTH GLORIOUS MYSTERY

*The Assumption
of Our Lady*

*I*n this woodcut, Mary seems already to be part of another world as she gazes toward heaven, her hands raised in prayer. The lilies by her side denote her purity, the star echoing the star of Bethlehem. The angels burn incense in her honor.

Very little if anything is known of the years that remained to Our Lady after the death and Resurrection of her Son. We know that she was with the disciples at Pentecost, and one tradition has it that she lived until the age of sixty-three. She is very likely to have lived peacefully among the disciples; and we can be certain that she prayed for the young Church.

We are left in complete ignorance of any words she may have spoken, for her words were recorded on only four occasions. The last reported words spoken by Mary were uttered at the marriage feast at Cana, when she responded to the needs of the hosts by speaking to her Son. Our Lady said to the servants: "Do whatever he tells you" (John 2:5). Throughout the entire New Testament, this is the only command Mary gives. Her eternal role as intercessor is underlined by her love for her Son and her loving concern for his creatures and the knowledge that only by doing his will can we be truly content. This single command tells us everything we need to know.

As a human being, Our Lady was bound by the laws of nature, and death is part of that law. As the one creature born without original sin, there was nothing to keep her in the grave; Satan held no sway whatsoever over this immaculate person.

Nowadays, "tradition" sometimes has a quaintly folksy image, but within the Church, Tradition refers to the teaching handed down from the apostles, from one generation to the next, in an unceasing chain. The traditional teaching of the Assumption of Mary had been accepted from time immemorial in both East and West. It has been a subject of meditation in the Glorious Mysteries of the rosary since the thirteenth century, long before the final seal of papal approval in the declaration of the Doctrine of the Assumption in 1950.

The Assumption of Our Lady is a great promise to humankind. Our Lady had to die, but she was assumed body and soul into heaven as we shall be. For her, there was no shadow of death, as her sinless state freed her from the grave. We must await the final day, but, forgiven through the sacrifice of Christ, we have the evidence of the Assumption to fill us with optimism and hope.

Prayer

Mother of Christ,
we rejoice in you,
created to be the wheat
for the bread of life.
When the dark winds and the rain
drove the harvest field to a storm of gold,
locked in His love
you were unique to God
among the multitudinous wheat,
the chosen grain for the Host.
Now,
the red sheaves are bound,
the grain sifted and threshed,
the wheat in the bread.
Now,
the Creator's hands
that sheltered you,
like a fended flame in the wind,
reach down from a heaven
of cloudless blue,
receiving you into Eternal Light.

AMEN.

The Crowning
of Our Lady and the
Glory of all the Saints

*J*n this final engraving, Our Lord gently and tenderly places the crown on his mother's bowed head. It is an image of inexpressible love. The only people to witness this intimate scene are the saints. How wonderful must have been that meeting between the Son and his mother. The Son who had been born in a stable, and had lived subject to her, and the mother who had never protested during the agonizing betrayal and the death of her Son that had taken place before her stricken eyes.

This decade of the rosary is devoted to the meeting between God and the one creature who so perfectly responded to his grace that she became the new Eve: the perfection of his creation who would restore all that had been lost in the Garden of Eden when the human race began its long straggling march to Calvary.

Perfection is almost impossible for most of us to imagine. So far is it from our comprehension that we have maneuvered the meaning into something more bearable and material, trivializing its real meaning. In the same way the word "divine" has been casually misplaced without understanding.

The angel Gabriel told us at the Annunciation that Mary was full of grace, and so completely in favor with God, that perhaps she was the only contemplative who never needed to place any "obstacle" between herself and the world in order to speak to God. How often we think that all we need is to find some peaceful oasis in order to escape the muddles that surround us, in this serene place, open our hearts to God.

The personality of Our Lady was so full of humility that she is never mentioned for herself, but only in relation to the actions of her Son. As the Mother of God, she is the most important woman there has ever been or ever will be. Paintings on the walls of the catacombs show her carrying the child

Jesus, and the early Christians gradually became aware of her significance and realized that her own glory was necessary in order to magnify the glory of her Son. Devotion to Mary increased and at the General Council held at Ephesus in 431, the term "Mother of God" (*Theotokos*) was decreed. Despite this accolade, Our Lady herself was all silence and humility; her glory lay in her relationship to her Son, not her title.

Our Lady is closer to God than all the hosts of angels and saints, and yet she is the most holy mother of all humanity to whom she has given her crown of the rosary. The future is in our hands, and how little we have to fear if within those hands are held the beads of the rosary.

Prayer

Mary,
Immaculate Love,
we bless you.
Because, though rooted in earth
as we are,
you opened your heart to God,
expanding and opening wide
to the heat of the sun
in your sinless heart,
you opened our hearts
to the light.
All generations bless you,
flower of our race.
We are crowned in you,
Queen of Heaven,
crowned with stars
by the hands of Christ.

AMEN.

About Anne Vail

Anne Vail is the author of *The Story of the Rosary* published by Harper San Francisco.

About Caryll Houselander

Born in England in 1901, Frances Caryll Houselander was baptized as a child, but abandoned the Catholic faith as a teenager. After attending art school, working at various jobs, and exploring many different religions, she returned to Catholicism in the 1920s. She told the story of her lapse and return in the autobiography, *A Rocking-Horse Catholic.*

Houselander's first book, *This War Is the Passion*, was published in 1941, followed by a steady stream of other books up until her death in 1954. Among her most popular books is *The Reed of God,* her classic meditation on the Virgin Mary.

Houselander was a mystic who saw the suffering and risen Christ in all persons, and her writing has served to inspire devotion to him and his mother.

About David Jones

David Jones was born in Kent in 1885. His talent has been described as the greatest dual talent since Blake, for David Jones's war poetry is among the finest written, and he is recognized as one of the most gifted and sensitive British watercolor painters of the twentieth century.

He returned from the First World War profoundly influenced by his experiences and was received into the Catholic Church in 1923. The following year he joined the sculptor and engraver Eric Gill, founder of the Guild of Saint Joseph and Saint Dominic at Ditchling in Sussex, with whom he shared an interest in the beauty of early Christian art.

With the freedom of his new-found faith, David Jones embarked on a series of wood engravings of religious subjects. In 1924, the *Child's Rosary Book* was privately printed at Ditchling, from which the wood engravings in this book are reproduced. They are a glowing example of his new conception of the nature of art. Not only as a Catholic, but as an artist, David Jones recognized and drew strength from the doctrine of the inseparability of spirit and matter, which is so particularly apt in the undertaking of the illustration of the mysteries of the rosary.

In these works the figures of the saints, and of Our Lady in particular, are engraved with tenderness and sympathy, the soldiers are reminiscent of those with whom he shared trench and billet on the Western Front in World War I, and the animals are drawn with almost Franciscan affection. These linear designs are the forerunner of his mature work, with its highly imaginative view of the world suffused with spirituality. David Jones died in 1974, and since then there has been a growing awareness of his extraordinary talent.